LET ME CHALLENGE YOU WITH

Your Personal Challenge

DR. SHARON LEE GRAHAM, D.C.COUN., Th.D.

McClure Publishing, Inc.

Copyright © 2015

Dr. Sharon Lee Graham, D.C.Coun., Th.D. for McClure Publishing, Inc.

Your Personal Challenge with Die-Hard Wealth and Prosperity

All rights reserved. Printed and bound in the United States of America. According to the 1976 United States Copyright Act, no portions of this workbook may be reproduced or utilized in any form or by any means, electronic or mechanical, including photocopying, recording, or by any information storage or retrieval system, except by a reviewer who may quote brief passages in a review to be printed in a magazine or newspaper, without permission in writing from the Publisher: Inquiries should be addressed to McClure Publishing, Inc. Permissions Department, 398 West Army Trail Road, Suite 124, Bloomingdale, Illinois 60108. First Printing: June 1, 2015.

The author and publisher have made every effort to ensure the accuracy and completeness of information contained in this book, we assume no responsibility for errors, inaccuracies, omissions, or any inconsistency therein.

Any slights of people, places, belief systems or organizations are unintentional. Any resemblance to anyone living, dead or somewhere in between is truly coincidental.

ISBN 978-09742237-2-8
0-9742237-2-7
LCCN: 2015942957
~~ 2nd Edition ~~
Cover Design and Interior Layout by Kathy McClure
McClure Publishing, Inc.
800.659.4908

To order additional copies, please contact
DR. SHARON LEE GRAHAM PRODUCTIONS
http://www.sharonleegraham.com/
and at
www.mcclurepublishing.com

TABLE OF CONTENTS

	Page
PURPOSE	5
KNOWING YOURSELF	7
TO SHARE OR NOT TO SHARE	8
YOUR MIND	14
THOUGHT PROVOKING QUESTIONS	18
THE PICTURE – THE MIND - THE SPIRIT	20
YOUR ENERGY – YOUR ATTITUDE – YOUR SUCCESS	26
A PRAYER	43
ABOUT THE AUTHOR	
NOTES	

WILL YOU LET ME CHALLENGE YOU TO FACE YOUR OWN PERSONAL CHALLENGES?

PURPOSE

The purpose of this book is to help give a boost of motivation to those who have something on the inside of them that is just waiting to leap out. That something is screaming, yelling, jumping up and down, and hoping someone will lend a hand, speak a word or do something that will set free that burst of energy, invention, imagination, something very valuable, whatever it may be. You have this something inside of you and you might know what it is or you might need help with identifying what it is, but you do know it is there…inside of you.

This book is for motivational purposes only and is not to be used for any type of diagnosis or treatment.

KNOWING YOURSELF

This book is going to be your book because it is going to be about you. There are some things you should know about yourself. Would you be surprised to find out that there are some things you do not know about yourself?

There have been times when circumstances have caused a quick reaction and we say something or do something we wish we had not said or had not done. What was said or done is out in the field of the atmosphere working to bring forth a mighty harvest. Whatever you hold in your heart will manifest when circumstances arise. Regardless of the type of circumstance, there will be some type of reaction. If good is in your heart, good will come out, if rage is in your heart, rage will come out. Circumstances bring about the realization of what is in you. So, do we know us? Let's make it personal. How much do you know about yourself? Do you like yourself? Do you know how to love yourself in a healthy way? Are there things in your past that cause you to feel the way you feel and think about yourself? How do you treat yourself? How do you treat others? How do you filter what you hear others say to or about you? How do you filter the way people look at you? There are hundreds of questions to be asked and answered in order to get to the root of you knowing a few things about yourself. We are going to cover a few items. You are a mystery and we would need the rest of eternity to continue learning who you are.

TO SHARE OR NOT TO SHARE

Why do you share some things about yourself with others and other things you would rather not? Do you share because you feel comfortable doing so or because you feel obligated? Some people seem to have a habit of prying, meddling and picking for information that you might not want to share. Most of the time, they know you are holding back information but they tend to be forceful in their attempt at getting your personal information. Is this person interviewing you for a high-paying job? Is this person a judge sitting on the bench and you are the person being questioned because you have been charged with a crime? Does this person have the right to question you? Are you required to answer the questions being asked? I am asking a lot of questions just because I want you to be prepared in advance with the answers you need to protect yourself from prying people whenever you are approached. Answer all of the questions asked on the previous page. Another question: Why do you think I am asking so many questions? The answer is on the previous page. Are you paying attention?

Remember, you are a mystery, you have challenges and you have rights. Do you feel the less people know about you the better off you are? Some people will answer no, and that is a good answer. Some people will answer yes, and that is a good answer. Did you really think I would take sides with either answer? Remember, too much information given to others can put you in a dangerous position. Can you think of reasons that would validate that statement? EXAMPLE: Your financial status could put you in danger of robbery if that information is given to the wrong person. What are some other reasons can you think of that could cause danger if too much information is given to those who do not have a need to know?

_____

_____

_____

Do you feel people will look at you in a different light if they knew the real you? Does it really matter to you? Why?

_____

_____

_____

_____

Someone might fall in love with the real you. Did you know that you are not required to spill your guts to the whole world? That being said, you need to face the truth even if it is painful. Can you think of truths that you have avoided but now you are ready to face?

_____

_____

_____

_____

I have faced many truths and have tasted the salt from the tears that never touched the cheeks of my face. The pain was so deep. I cried inside and wanted to back out of facing the pain I felt. I made it through the process that was needed to get me set free. I am free and it feels good. Face the pain and get free. You will be glad you did.

If you feel the need to make changes to certain areas in your life, you can choose to make the necessary changes and move forward. You are to be in charge of what gets changed in your life. Never allow what others do or say to or about you dictate your actions or the way you feel about yourself, doing so would be giving them too much power and control over your life. Do not think low of your own self; you can pull yourself down if you allow yourself to do so. You have the power and authority to speak prosperity over your own life.

So, bless yourself and recognize who you are. You are a mystery.

Take the time to bless yourself:

_____

_____

LET ME CHALLENGE YOU WITH YOUR PERSONAL CHALLENGE

_____

_____

_____

_____

_____

_____

_____

_____

YOUR PHOTO HERE

Let me challenge you to picture yourself being where you want to be. Place a photo of yourself in the space provided on the previous page. Remember, this is your book because this book is about you.

YOUR MIND

You have a great mind. Your mind works constantly, even when you are not aware of the many activities taking place in your mind. Your mind plays a vital role concerning your daily activities. You are able to function properly if your mind is functioning properly. Having a mental picture is very important when you want to accomplish something. A mental picture of what you desire is helpful for envisioning things that you do not have physically, for helping you accomplish things that you do not know how to accomplish, for helping you to obtain whatever you need when you don't have what you think you need to accomplish it, whatever it is, but you have an imagination of what the outcome could be, should be or would be.

In your mind you can picture the greatness of your accomplishment and the satisfaction you could have, should have or would have. Do not look to be amused all of the time. The TV and radio are used for amusement. Let us learn to muse more than being amused all of the time. Do not get me twisted, I like amusement, but I also like to muse. I like to work my intellect. I like to use my mind. You will find out how much intelligence you were blessed with as you quiet yourself and think of the many virtuous things you are capable of accomplishing. What inventions are you sitting on? Be sure to muse about your talents and passions. Let your real values come forth. It is your time. Use your mind and never forget to acknowledge the Lord in all you do, and remember to seek the mind of the Spirit before you do anything. Real success and happiness will come your way when you put God first.

If I wanted to build a custom made boat, I would need to capture it in my mind through my imagination and then have it drawn on paper so I could see it. In my mind, I would imagine the shape, size, color and unique features that I have not been able to capture from any other boat that I have seen. My boat would be custom made to my specifications. I have wild imaginations. How about you? My boat would probably fly. How about yours?

You have seen boats. I have seen boats. Boats were in existence before we were born, so we can more easily make changes in our minds and say we are going to custom make our own boat. Now, on the other hand, what about something that you have never seen, never heard of, but there is something in your mind and you can feel a tugging in your spirit about this something that you cannot explain because you have never seen this thing, you don't know if it exists, and you don't know what to call it? I have experienced this and I know I am not the only person with this experience.

What experiences have you had in this area? What actions have you taken concerning these experiences?

_____

_____

_____

_____

_____

_____

THOUGHT PROVOKING QUESTIONS

You are a valuable vessel and a gift from the Lord. We need you. The world is waiting for you to share that valuable thing that has been deposited on the inside of you.

Do you recognize your value? What are some of the gifts and talents you have for the benefit of others?

_____

_____

_____

_____

List some of the skills and several abilities you have?

_____

LET ME CHALLENGE YOU WITH YOUR PERSONAL CHALLENGE

_____

_____

_____

Why are you gifted and talented, for yourself or others? Why do you have skills and abilities? Are you selfish and unwilling to share your talents or unwilling to use the gift God gave you to enhance others? What will you do to fulfill the purpose of having all of these bestowed upon you?

_____

_____

_____

THE PICTURE – THE MIND - THE SPIRIT

Having a mental picture of where you want to be, and positive thoughts, along with The Holy Spirit of God leading the way, will lead to success if you continue through the process. In order to get something done, you must first get started. Some people can never get started and some people are good starters but never get finished. My prayer is that those who can never seem to get started will get the boost, courage and assurance they need to get started and that the starters will get the revelation that they will reap the harvest of the work they have begun if they continue and finish it. All of the work can be successfully accomplished if God is acknowledged and given the credit that is due to Him. Knowledge, strength, ability, power and endurance come from Our Heavenly Father, The Almighty!

Remember, you can do what you set your mind to do. Start imagining what you want to do. What do you want to do: Is it your passion? Is it something that is burning inside of you? Was it a suggestion by someone else?

Now that you know it is important to have an imagination concerning where you want to go, I want you to look at the photo of yourself. I want you to see yourself, not just a photo, but I want you to see yourself and picture yourself going where you want to go. Where do you want to go?

_____

_____

_____

_____

Do you want to go to a comfortable place where others have already been and have already succeeded and you feel you can succeed because someone else succeeded? A word to the wise: Just because someone else succeeded does not necessarily mean you will succeed. You must follow your calling in life, not someone else's.

Look at your photo. This is your book. It is all about you. You are a mystery. Let's find out more about you.

How do you like the photo you chose?

_____

_____

_____

_____

Why did you choose this photo?

_____

_____

_____

Did you choose this photo because others like it?

LET ME CHALLENGE YOU WITH YOUR PERSONAL CHALLENGE

_____

_____

_____

_____

How you look at yourself is very important in many ways. How you look at yourself helps to determine how you treat yourself, how you present yourself to others and how you are perceived and received by others. How you look at yourself determines what you think about yourself. When you look in the mirror or look at your photo, do you frown or smile at yourself? The answer to this question counts significantly in the challenge of picturing yourself being where you want to be.

Look at the photo again. Are there changes you would like to make? (Hair style, makeup, smile, outfit, etc.?) Maybe you like your photo the way it is. No changes.

_____

_____

_____

_____

Are there any other changes you would like to work on? (Attitude, disposition, hospitality, habits, etc.?)

_____

_____

_____

_____

When you look at yourself, do you see negative attitudes or bad habits, and you hope no one else can see these negatives? What are they? Are you willing to work on them? What are some of the ways you will change the negative to positive? When will you start?

_____

_____

_____

_____

_____

_____

_____

When you look at yourself, do you see attitudes that you recognize to be healthy for yourself and for those who come in contact with you and you want others to see the energy of these good attitudes? What are they? What are you willing to do to cause this energy to spread?

_____

_____

_____

_____

YOUR ENERGY – YOUR ATTITUDE – YOUR SUCCESS

If you are an energized person with a healthy attitude that is targeted in the right direction with the right motive and the right spirit, you can accomplish what you attempt to do while encouraging others to do the same.

Healthy thoughts about yourself will take you far. Take the time to search deep within yourself. What is your purpose in life? Do you know? Have you asked the Lord about it?

_____

_____

_____

_____

_____

_____

_____

Do you believe there is something in life that you are assigned to accomplish? Do you know what it is? What is it? Have you asked the Lord about it? What did He say? Are you acting upon it or are you hesitating?

_____

_____

_____

_____

_____

_____

_____

_____

What is your vision concerning where you want to be? When do you want to be there? Have you set a goal for how you will get there and how long you anticipate it will take for you to get there?

_____

_____

LET ME CHALLENGE YOU WITH YOUR PERSONAL CHALLENGE

_____

_____

_____

_____

_____

_____

_____

After answering the following question, look at your photo and picture yourself being where you want to be. You can be there. You have a mental and physical picture to keep tucked deep in your spirit and to look at. Talk to yourself. Talk to your photo. Pray to the Father in Jesus' name. Listen to the voice of God's Holy Spirit and obey Him.

What is your dream concerning where you picture yourself being? You can dream big!

_____

_____

_____

_____

_____

_____

_____

God gives dreams, too. You can accomplish God-given dreams concerning your purpose in life. There is a purpose for your existence. You are not just a blob. You are not just a piece of matter that takes up space and has weight. You are very valuable. God has placed something very valuable in you and He is looking for a return on His investment.

Are you willing to give yourself to Him? When? Where? How? He is waiting for you.

_____

_____

_____

_____

Concerning the challenge, **"picture yourself being where you want to be,"** and after reading, giving thought and answering questions, have you any additional input as to where you want to be?

_____

_____

_____

_____

_____

_____

Since you have indicated the place you picture yourself being, have you started toward getting there?

_____

_____

_____

_____

Have you run into road blocks? What were they? (Placing blame is immature.)

_____

_____

_____

_____

_____

_____

_____

How did you overcome them? Are they still there?

_____

_____

_____

_____

_____

_____

_____

Whenever you attempt to fulfill your purpose, realize that there is always an opposing force standing by.

That is a fact. You must also realize that the truth is, you can overcome the opposing force and accomplish your calling if you obey God, set your mind to your purpose and do not stop or get weary of doing what you are called to do.

Whatever that something is that is inside of you leaping, screaming, jumping up and down and longing to be discovered, you must move forward to release it. You will not be fulfilled without the release.

Write your feelings concerning the thing or things you feel burning inside of you and you know there needs to be a release before you are fulfilled. Without fulfilling your purpose, there is no feeling of fulfillment. When did you first realize there was something or some things inside of you that you need to accomplish?

_____

_____

_____

_____

_____

_____

_____

What assistance do you need to get started with the process of getting these things accomplished? Do you need someone to pray with you? Do you need to network with people of like faith, interests, skills, talents, etc.? Do you need information concerning the area you are pursuing? Do you need a word spoken over you? Do you need a helping hand to help with extra duties involved with your dream? Do you need to get involved with a group of people who are accomplished, busy and business-minded and know how to get things done? List some of the people, groups or resources that you feel would be an asset to help you accept the challenge of being where you have pictured yourself, whether your challenge involves business, family, finance, lifestyle or any other challenge not mentioned?

_____

_____

_____

_____

Surround yourself with confidence and take note of who surrounds you. You might discover the need to change your surroundings as well as some who surround you.

What skills, talents, abilities and knowledge do you have that you would want the world to benefit from your sharing with them?

_____

_____

_____

_____

_____

_____

_____

You have listed things that will benefit others. How can you get the word out concerning the above list?

_____

_____

_____

_____

_____

_____

_____

_____

_____

Take a look at your photo. Would you make changes to anything about you yet? This is just a question to be used as a periodic check and it is not intended to make you feel you need to change anything about yourself. This is your book because it is about you and don't you ever forget it!

There are role models in our lives, some on TV, some on the radio, some at school, some in sports, some in church, etc. People influence us in many different ways, even when we are not aware of being influenced. There might have been someone who was a sharp dresser whom we admired and later on in life, for some reason, we place a strong emphasis on dressing sharp. Was it because we were influenced by the sharp dresser? Do you have things in the past that cause you to feel like you feel about yourself? Try to think of both positive influences as well as negative influences. Which influences are hindering you and which influences are helping you? Which ones do you need to rid yourself of and which ones do you want to keep and build upon?

_____

_____

_____

_____

_____

_____

_____

_____

_____

Recognize who you are. You are a mystery and your challenge might be very personal and intimate. Your challenge might be the need to be rid of addictions or other lifestyle habits that have negative effects on you and those around you. You face your challenges alone at times. Maybe you have not shared certain challenges with others for fear of what they will say or think about you. I want to say to you that, "you can overcome and win the victory you desire if you want to." Review and answer all of the thought-provoking questions in this book. I challenge you to obey God and then picture yourself where you want to be. This is the real challenge: Obeying God. Come to Jesus and learn of Him. This is how you find rest from your weariness. He made you to be the mystery that you are. He did a marvelous job.

Place another photo of yourself on the following page. Will you use the same photo? Give yourself the reason for using the photo you are using.

_____

_____

_____

_____

Will you accept the challenge of picturing yourself in your book and seeing yourself being where you want to be? Realize there is a price to pay, but the price is worth it.

Being where you are called to be is where your desire should be. God will give you the desire and He will grant you the grace to fulfill the desire.

I accepted the challenge and I will continue to accept the challenges that lead to fulfilling God's plan for my life.

One last thought-provoking question for you: Will you accept the challenge?

A PRAYER

My heavenly Father, I bless your most holy and awesome name. I worship you and honor your presence. You mean more than life to me. I thank you for loving me, protecting me and for holding me dear to your heart. The Bible tells me that your plan for me is a good plan, and that your plan is for my good, to do me good all the days of my life and not evil. Your plan is for me to receive the promise of a good future and a good end. Your plan is for the earth to be inhabited with mankind; those who will fulfill your plan. I open my heart to you and ask that you impart unto me godly wisdom, knowledge, understanding, skills and abilities that will enable me to carry out your desire for my life.

I give myself to you and depend on the leading, teaching and comfort of the Holy Spirit. Thank you for being such a merciful, loving Father. I thank you in advance for giving me grace to be merciful and loving to those who show me love and mercy and to those who do not. Thank you for providing everything I need and more. The Bible tells me that it is your pleasure to give me the kingdom. You have always been my help, strength and protector. You have done more for me than I could ever say. What can I render to you for all you have done for me? I give you myself, my life and all that I have. Use me, my Lord, to fulfill your plan and purpose for my life. I surrender all, as I wait to hear from you, in Jesus' name. Amen!

ABOUT THE AUTHOR

Dr. Sharon Lee Graham is an author, business woman, and pastor. She strives to do business and ministry in the spirit of excellence and believes in keeping her word, even if it hurts or causes her to put forth an extra effort. She emphasizes that operating in the spirit of excellence and keeping your word are two of the most important things you can do if you expect to gain respect and trust in ministry or business.

Dr. Graham is a native of Chicago, Illinois, and has lived in the state of Illinois most of her life. She attended schools in the Chicago area and majored in the field of business. Dr. Graham has worked for numerous companies throughout the years, including the Federal Aviation Administration (FAA). She retired from the FAA with more than 37 years of public service. Due to the training received, she has held various positions and is well-rounded in many areas of aviation and business. She is fully aware of how the training and experiences in life have prepared her for the future; they are the stepping stones that continue leading her to higher heights in her business and ministry.

In 2000, while working full-time and overseeing two non-profit ministries, Dr. Graham attended the Christian Satellite Bible University, Chicago, Illinois, where she majored in Christian Counseling. In 2001 she received her degree of Bachelor of Christian Education in Christian Counseling graduating class valedictorian, Summa Cum Laude; in 2002 she received her Master Degree graduating Summa Cum Laude, and in 2004 she received her Doctoral Degree graduating Summa Cum Laude. She continued her education and earned her Doctoral Degree in Theology in 2006, graduating Summa Cum Laude. These degrees were earned through the

International Apostolic University of Grace and Truth, Indianapolis, Indiana (IAUGT).

Dr. Graham has held the position of assistant pastor and has sat under the teachings of profound Bible scholars. Receiving her first license for ministry in 1966, she was publicly ordained in 1995. She is the Pastor of Life In Christ~Christ In Me Ministries, Inc., (April 1997), and president of Sharon Graham Ministries, Inc., (April 2003), located in a western suburb of Chicago.

Dr. Graham is the sole proprietor of Dr. Sharon Lee Graham Productions, a company that produces written materials, and has expectations of expanding the company by producing visual and audio materials as well. She loves to study and teach what she has learned. Dr. Graham seeks to motivate others by giving them a boost of encouragement and by pushing them forward and causing them to press ahead in the Spirit to the next level of where they are supposed to be.

She has written two other books that have been published, "How to Survive a Marriage with a Non-Christian Spouse," and a workbook "Your Personal Challenge With Die-Hard Wealth And Prosperity". Dr. Graham believes you must use what you have or you lose it. She said, "I am going to redeem the time and recover all. I do not have time to waste anything."

Let Me Challenge You With Your Personal Challenge

Contact information:

Website - www.sharonleegraham.com

Email - drslgproductions@sbcglobal.net

Dr. Sharon Lee Graham Productions, Copyright June 2015

NOTES

LET ME CHALLENGE YOU WITH YOUR PERSONAL CHALLENGE

LET ME CHALLENGE YOU WITH YOUR PERSONAL CHALLENGE

www.ingramcontent.com/pod-product-compliance
Lightning Source LLC
Chambersburg PA
CBHW061120010526
44112CB00024B/2924